SUPER DUPER CLOSE UP

# SUPER DUPER CLOSE UP

A Made In China production
created by Jessica Latowicki

OBERON BOOKS
LONDON

WWW.OBERONBOOKS.COM

First published in 2018 by Oberon Books Ltd
521 Caledonian Road, London N7 9RH
Tel: +44 (0) 20 7607 3637 / Fax: +44 (0) 20 7607 3629
e-mail: info@oberonbooks.com
www.oberonbooks.com



A catalogue record for this book is available from the British Library.

PB ISBN: 9781786826862
E ISBN: 9781786826855

Cover design by James Illman

Printed and bound by 4EDGE Limited, Hockley, Essex, UK.
eBook conversion by Lapiz Digital Services, India.



Printed on FSC accredited paper

10 9 8 7 6 5 4 3 2 1

*For my family, especially my not long-lost, super fabulous aunt, Bella.*

**Made In China** make theatre that playfully explores the paradoxes of modern identity, inspired by the unique collaboration between Tim Cowbury and Jessica Latowicki. Dynamic, devious, visually arresting, verbally sharp performances and projects that jump in at deep ends to find new ways of probing what it feels like to be alive now. Work that challenges dominant assumptions and structures of the ailing west, asking how and why we tell stories in a world overloaded with stories. Funny, sad, provocative stuff to witness and be part of, for anyone who looks at the world and is confused, amused, perturbed or downright angry.

**Made In China**

**Acknowledgements**

Thanks to the people who went out of their way to help this thing come into being: Jay Miller and everyone at The Yard, Christina Elliot, Matt Burman and Daniel Kok, Eugénie Pastor (for your excellent French), Christopher Brett Bailey, Ben Harvey and John Hunter. Thank you to the brilliant team of artists who collaborated with me – without you, this would literally be nothing but nonsense. Thanks to Sophie Oliver for reading every single draft and pointing me towards all of the best women, to Susan Butler for being famille choisie and to Nayana Crowe for being the littlest muse.

As always, thanks to Danny, Kitty, Monica, Michael and Devon for being my light in all of this darkness.

Extra special thank you to Beckie Darlington who held my hand, wiped away my tears and produced the shit out of the show.

And I'd especially like to thank Tim for holding my heart so lovingly – without you everything would be grey.

**Note on the text**

*Super Duper Close Up* is Made In China's seventh show, but until now we've resisted publishing our texts. Until now, it's been questionable whether it makes sense to. So far, the shows have been drawn quite personally from the specific individuals (including performers) who've made the show; and designed for the original performers to be the only-ever performers. Text has always been one of several equally-weighted strands that make up a show. Maybe it's always the case that a text can't really capture the essence of a live experience; but when physical tasks, endurance, spatial constraints and aesthetic are as key to meaning as they have been for us, all the more so.

*Super Duper Close Up* is mostly no different. It draws on real life but also fictionalises wildly. It's absolutely a show meant to be performed only by me. The real physical tasks and visual world up on stage are crucial to the audience experience. But it's by miles the densest thing Made In China have ever done, and the first written exclusively by one of us. For the first time, reading the text is perhaps as rewarding (in its own way) as watching the show. We've given almost no clues to what actually happens on stage in the following pages, resisting the temptation to turn it into a play with stage directions. So I guess, taking a deep breath: make of it what you will.

*Jessica Latowicki, November 2018.*

*Super Duper Close Up* opened at The Yard Theatre on 13 November 2018.

*Creator & Performer:* Jessica Latowicki

*Dramaturg:* Tim Cowbury

*Camera Person & Performer:* Valentina Formenti

*Music & Sound Designer:* Tom Parkinson

*Designer:* Emma Bailey

*Design Assistant:* Lauren Dix

*Video Designer:* Mikaela Liakata

*Lighting Designer:* Alex Fernandes

*Choreographer:* Irene Cioni

*Production Manager:* Simon Perkins

*Producer:* Beckie Darlington

Commissioned by Cambridge Junction, The Yard Theatre, and Theatre in the Mill. Supported using public funding by the National Lottery through Arts Council England. With thanks to Theatre Deli and Battersea Arts Centre.

On a Tuesday, not so long ago but also not this year, I went in for a meeting.

It was a pretty normal meeting. It wasn't about anything special.
Not a meeting of any note.
I didn't think that I would come out of the meeting with anything more than I went into the meeting with.
Unless of course, I did.
Ultimately, I was meeting this person because I wanted them to give me something that I didn't have.
Money.
Or time.
Or space.

But this meeting wasn't actually about asking for those things. Even if those things are the things that I was ultimately hoping I would get.

It was more of the kind of meeting where I was checking in.

With the person I was meeting.

We were checking in with each other about where we both were. About where we had both been. About where we each were going and whether we thought there might be a way we could go there together.

Metaphorically, of course. The where is a metaphor. It's a metaphor for money. Or time. Or space.

A couple of my friends, a couple, Kate and Victor, got married recently. I went to the wedding. In their speeches to each other, their vows, they spent a lot of time talking about where they were going – and of course when they talked about that, they were both speaking about a metaphor and actual places they'll go. Kate and Victor like to travel and both have jobs that have international offices or placements or something. They spent last year in Portland and they are thinking of going to New Zealand next winter, after their honeymoon. I like this couple, I think they're a good pair. They look very similar, like if they said they were related you'd believe them. Sometimes Kate invites her brother, Duncan, along to social events, like dinner or trips to the pub, or even festivals – and whenever Duncan is there, or whenever Kate posts photos of Duncan and Victor together on social media, I always think to myself how similar Duncan and Victor look as well. I thought that at the wedding. As Kate and Victor were talking about all of the places they promise to take each other, metaphorically and literally, I was thinking about how basically everyone in their families all could be related. By blood.

And then I thought how good they'd all look when they inevitably posted a photo online. Not only would their ties and dresses and like, corsages all match, their faces would too.

I was early for the meeting. I'm early for everything. I used to think it was a hangover from when I smoked. I'd get places early so I'd have time to have a cigarette. But really, the reason I like being early is because it gives me a moral high ground, especially if the person I am meeting is running late. Waiting patiently is virtuous. And being late is stressful. And life is already stressful enough. I was early for my meeting so I was trying to focus on a crossword puzzle. I do a lot of crossword puzzles. I read it's an excellent way to strength your ability to recall the right word in the right situation. It's part of my concerted effort to be less … um.

But also, I do the crossword because otherwise I spend all my downtime looking at photos. On my phone.

This meeting I was going to, it was rescheduled four times. I rescheduled it the first time because I double booked myself.

The other three times Harriet rescheduled. That's who I was meeting. Harriet. This meeting between Harriet and myself, had been a long time in the making. Countless emails, a handful of texts, and one last minute phone call, which happened when I had already arrived at the venue, the last time we were supposed to meet.

The venue is obviously referring to the building where the meeting takes place. Harriet works at this venue. And as you can probably tell, I make work for venues.

The meeting itself wasn't about a particular work. It was about the possibility of work. About whether there was a possibility that the building Harriet worked at would be interested in working with me, providing me with space to work so that I could make a work that would work for them.

Harriet was late.
And I was early.

I was early enough that I moved from my crossword puzzle to scrolling through an entirely visual social media app. You might know the one I mean. It's pretty addictive, right? Sometimes I dip in for a quick scroll and then suddenly realise I've been looking, mindlessly, for twenty-three and a half minutes and I've missed my stop on the bus and it's nighttime so there isn't another one for like thirty-five minutes so I end up having to walk all the way back like a mile – in the rain. You know?

I stopped the crossword because it was hard – I can still really only do Monday and Tuesday without having to look up every answer. They get progressively harder as the week goes on and I'm still a crossword novice after three years of pretty regular crosswording.

I feel like I've gotten worse at retaining or recalling information, so even if I sort of know what something is, I often can't, you know… find it.

I worry sometimes that this is a warning sign of Alzheimer's. I'm in my thirties, and apparently, there can be warning signs this early. Plus my grandfather had Alzheimer's. He died when I was very young, so it's hard for me to know if he also displayed signs, like forgetting names of television shows or forgetting being introduced to people or forgetting appointments even when they're in your calendar. Sometimes, when I can't sleep, I try to remember each detail of my day – everything I said, everything I saw, all the breaks I took, everything I read and listened to, all the new things I learned from the crossword – to make sure my brain is still working the best it can.

My grandfather, his life was very hard. His life had been so hard that he didn't want to remember things. He wanted to forget. He prayed and prayed and prayed to forget things that happened in his life. Maybe he wished the Alzheimer's into existence. Maybe each time he prayed, a small part of his brain would disappear, a small memory or word or sound. And so eventually he forgot everything.

He drooled a lot, when he was sick. My grandfather. I got a little scared of him then.

My life, it's not been that hard and I don't want to forget anything. But I do anyway.

That's a lie. There are actually some things that I'd like to forget. But those are the things I seem to remember. They never seem to leave. In fact, they seem to get stronger. Maybe those bad memories are eating the memories that I want to keep or the words I am trying to remember. You know, like Pacman. The bad memories are using up all my storage! And I can't work out how to erase them.

The crossword was too hard. Sometimes Tuesdays are just right and sometimes they're just out of reach and it really has to do with how much I've slept and whether I did my brain exercises and my body drills and what I know and what I need to learn today and while I was sat in the reception of the staff entrance to the venue waiting for Harriet I didn't seem to know anything. And I was frustrated which was frustrating because I didn't want to be frustrated at the start of a meeting that wasn't about much in particular, more just about working out whether work would work which is already frustrating enough.

So, I started scrolling.

Apparently, scrolling releases dopamine in our brain – that's why it's so addictive. Did you know that when dogs lick us, it's the same – dopamine is released in their brains. That's why they do it. Lick us. That and our skin is salty and it probably tastes nice.

It is Tuesday and I am sitting waiting to go into a professional meeting where Harriet, the person I am meeting, will talk about themselves for a while, then I will talk about work and then Harriet will say something to me that I will not be able to forget. Despite trying.

But I don't know that yet. For now, I am scrolling, breathing deeply, wishing I still was a regular smoker.

When Kate and Victor got married I smoked. Even though I don't really smoke anymore. I had to keep asking people for cigarettes. I asked Duncan, Kate's brother, for quite a lot of cigarettes. He seemed to always be outside engaging different female wedding guests in intense chat. Duncan is a toucher, like, he always touches your arm when you speak to him. And he's a quite close talker. You sort of always get the impression when he's speaking that he could kiss you at any time. Everyone thinks that. Even all the married people who were there, even the ones who'd brought their tiny shiny new children along, I could tell they were like woah are you leaning in for a kiss?

I'm not married. I'd like to be. No. It's not that I'd like to be married, I just want to have the wedding. I do all the stuff that I would do if was married already. I live with my boyfriend, we have a shared bank account and one day we'll maybe even have a human baby together. But I like weddings. And I like parties.

I mean, also, maybe it would be horrible. To have a wedding. I like parties but I don't really like throwing them. I am always worried no one is going to come. I'm also worried people are going to come but they are going to have a really awful time. The thought of having a party that no one came to, or that people came to but it was boring, or people did come to the party but they were the wrong people, is so awful that my palms are actually starting to sweat even thinking about it.

It's Tuesday.
A year or two ago. It's a very average Tuesday.
I'm early.

I'm scrolling.

And sitting.

I was feeling pleased with myself momentarily for getting the answer to the crossword clue 'Odysseus' spouse', and I was wondering what it would be like if I could knit. Or weave. Like a shawl.

I was wondering if having an activity like that, like weaving or knitting, or even crocheting … or cross-stitching even … would help me avoid distractions.

I was wondering this and also trying to mentally prepare for the meeting I was waiting for.

And I couldn't remember the name of the person who made the work that Harriet had just worked on. I had even been along to see the work, and I couldn't remember the guy's name. It was really starting to bother me and I didn't want to look it up because I don't want to rely on my phone to tell me the answer to all the things I can't immediately remember because, according to the short introduction/information essay that came with my brain exercises, the more I do that, the more my ability to to to to … *recall* information will become less sharply attuned.

So I didn't look it up, the name of the guy who made the work that Harriet worked on. Instead, I stopped scrolling and looked up "can't recall names early onset Alzheimer's thirties warning signs" and then, without paying much attention to what the search results were, I searched "early Alzheimer warning signs thirties genetic runs in family". Then "Alzheimer Ashkenazi Jews early warning" then "if my grandfather had Alzheimer's how likely am I to get it percentage" followed by "how long does it take for Alzheimer's to kick in thirties early on-set" and finally "best haircuts bob round face one length".

I used to have very short hair. I cut it on a whim when I was having a bad day working. My hair had been very very long, and then I cut it to a medium length and then I cut it all off. And then, I grew it out very very long again, until I just recently cut it. It took me four years to do that, to grow it out very very long again. Not because it doesn't grow fast, it does, but because I'm impatient and bleached it and it fell out a little bit I had to cut it again. I didn't bleach it myself. A trendy salon near where I live did – they are sort of famous for Kool-aide hair – they – the person who did my hair there – bleached over the bleach line and it all fell out and they didn't care because I wasn't a person of interest.

A person of influence I mean.

So I cut it off and started again and it took forever. Because I also kept bleaching it.

I like to change my hair a lot. It's probably because I don't want to be recognized. On the street. By people I know.

Harriet, she has very nice hair, it always looks like she's had an expensive haircut. Her hair is not so different to mine. She actually looks relatively similar to me. In that we are both white women over thirty with shortish hair. We are different in that she is from this place we are both living in and I am not, her hair it's gray, more like actually a really nice silver, one you can't fake you just have to be a genetic winner, she is nearly fifteen years older than me, she has children, she is married, I assume she owns her property and she has a job, which obviously I also have, but my work is rewarded, shall we say … differently … So by job what I really mean is that she has a salary.

Also, she's quite tall. That's different too.

I've known Harriet for a while now. The first ten times we met she literally didn't remember me. And now, every time she sees me – at a professional party or a work event or just sort of around she exclaims quite loudly "I never recognize you, your hair is always different!" even if it was the same last time I saw her. Harriet is someone who I both try to avoid and try to speak to, depending on how I am feeling. I sometimes find myself in situations … where … umm … I don't know. I just don't want to be seen. Where I feel myself … wanting to disappear.

And I wonder why I left the house at all.

I was early at this place of work, this place where Harriet works to help people's work get made and I was scrolling and searching. I was waiting for Harriet, and thinking about waiting. Thinking about Penelope, sitting waiting on the island of Ithaca while Odysseus was, you know, off sailing and fighting and fucking and tricking. Except she wasn't just sitting waiting, she had to be clever too, and defend her palace from the suitors who were like …

circling. Like vultures. I didn't have any suitors, I just had my phone. So I carried on scrolling and I scrolled onto a photo of a beautiful young French woman – a French woman of influence – who is famous for being beautiful and taking photos, basically. In the photo, she's actually in Ithaca, the island, and she's wearing a T-shirt that says Ithaca is gorges. Like, canyons. Gorges. But I'm thinking, that T-shirt isn't referring to the Greek island, it's referring to a University town in upstate New York. Where there are a lot of gorges. I felt better about myself for like a second – I felt like somehow I had the upper hand. Like somehow for just a second, I was better.

But the reality was, this very beautiful person was on a very beautiful beach on an actually mythical island and I was sat in a hallway waiting for my meeting with Harriet. Who was running late.

There is a moment, where this happened – where I stopped being early and Harriet started being late. This moment, is precisely five minutes after the time we agreed to meet. I was there seven minutes before the time we agreed to meet so when Harriet became late I had been there for twelve minutes. I've been talking now for around fifteen minutes.

Harriet was going to be another thirteen minutes. So she finally arrived eighteen minutes behind our scheduled meeting time, thirteen minutes after the buffer window ended and twenty-five minutes after I got to the venue.

The buffer window isn't a real thing. I made it up because I find being late so stressful. I am almost always early but on the off chance I'm not, I need to give myself a little bit of leeway.

I am always trying to find ways to minimize feeling panicked. It's very easy for a small amount of panic to escalate. Sometimes, it's a scale. Like

I am late.

My lateness will reflect badly on me with whomever this person is I am meeting.

I already have to try hard to make people like me.

I am an inherently unlikable person.

I am getting older and can't rely on my looks.

I've never been that good looking.

My teeth grinding and clenching is making my face look like I've had a stroke.

What if I have had a minor stroke and just didn't' notice.

Maybe I am unable to notice these things because I have another terrible illness.

It's very likely I have a terrible illness.

Apparently Ashkenazi Jews have a higher risk of breast cancer and I don't know my family medical history because everyone died in the Holocaust and I've been having numbness in my right arm and there is maybe some dimpling on my breast skin and I've definitely had a stroke and I can't remember the name of the work Harriet worked on and I'm probably going to die of a disease in the next three – sixty-five years.

If I don't die in a terrorist attack first.

The buffer window helps to mitigate this.
It doesn't prevent it.

Harriet didn't arrive until thirteen minutes after the buffer window had passed.

I sort of didn't care. That she was late. Or that I was so early.
That's a lie. I wish I was the kind of person that didn't care.
But I did care. And I had to pretend not to.
Because this meeting, the meeting I was about to have – in this meeting I wanted something. Harriet also wanted something. But the things we wanted were different. I didn't know what Harriet wanted, she didn't tell me. But Harriet knew that I wanted work. Or I wanted some space, in her venue. And some money. Some means. With which to produce something. To work.

I usually work in my living room, often just sitting on the couch, which is fine but it's easy to get distracted there.

And believe it or not I get distracted very easily anyway. I can't remember if that was always the case or if that is a new thing that has happened with the advent of scrolling? I find that when I am working or reading or even just writing emails, it is hard for me to stay focused for more than a few minutes on any one given thing. When I watch TV with my boyfriend he gets angry, he's always getting angry with me, but here he's angry that I always half watch the TV and half look on my phone or even worse, at a magazine. I do occasionally still buy magazines. I find the flicking even more soothing than the scrolling. But I can't justify the magazines, they are expensive and wasteful. And I never get rid of them, so they just build up like a monument of trash along with all the other crap I buy.

I read somewhere, recently, that shopping is an act of creativity. A writer I like wrote that. She said that when writing is going well she doesn't need to shop but when it's going badly she shops all the time. And I thought about that. I thought about that for an hour. I sat on my couch and looked at my things, the furniture I've bought, the pictures on the wall, the candles and knick-knacks, the lamps, the plastic lawn flamingo standing on a shelf, the clothes on the drying rack, the books and the shoes and plants and the small horses on the window sill and the large male mannequin and the bed and mattress and sheets, the beauty products and make-up and hair dryer and cleaning supplies and cloth shopping bags and leather handbags and exercise paraphernalia and record player and cups and glasses and pots and pans and the wall shelf for the pots and pan and the TV. I sat on my couch looked at all of this … shit … I've bought. And I thought. I thought about money. And I thought about art. And I thought about shoes.

And then I went online and bought a pair of gold hoop earrings. I don't wear a lot of jewelry but Kate wore these gold hoops at her wedding and I've been after a pair ever since.
She is very stylish, Kate.

Everything she wears looks good on her.

Victor likes taking photos of her.

He likes to document their lives.

And she likes to share.

Often when I'm scrolling I'll see photos they put up. Sometimes they share everyday photos like them in their house or trips to the pub. Sometimes they share photos from their travels or special events.

But, they don't ever put up photos of themselves working, even though I know they do work. I'm not 100% sure what their jobs are. Their work doesn't define them. That came up at the wedding. Their jobs aren't extensions of themselves, they feel fulfilled by friends and family and travelling and participating in cultural activities. That's an actual quote. Duncan said it in his speech. I remember it exactly because everyone laughed and I wasn't sure why.

But also.

Someone posted a short video of it; the speech. They found it of interest and thought other people might as well. So, I checked the post to make sure I remembered it correctly. I did.

But we all work, one way or another, don't we. My work is to make work and Harriet's work for example, is to facilitate people who do the kind of work I do to make work that will work for the place that she works and Kate and Victor work also but no one really knows what their work is. And maybe it doesn't matter, maybe that's the point: their work is only important in so far as it pays for the rest of their life, and sometimes I wonder if I misunderstood things drastically at some point years ago and in fact, that's all work is ever for.

I was sat on my couch after I bought the earrings, really trying remember what Kate and Victor's jobs were. I decided not to google them because I wanted to use the power of my memory and strengthen my ability recall information. At this exact time, I was also attempting to do some work whist looking at a newspaper article about a politician, AND simultaneously reading a think piece about a popular television show. The show had recently come out with a second season, so, there were a number of think pieces on it. Think pieces. Think pieces. All of the think pieces said the same thing. That it was torture porn. I read three different think pieces that used the phrase torture porn. Torture porn.

Torture porn. It could mean what it meant in these think pieces. Think pieces. Torture porn. That we are watching something violent and getting pleasure out of watching it but it isn't really porno porn. But. It could also mean porno porn that has torture in it. Very violent porn. Torture porn. Torture porn in this context isn't porno porn but is very violent and doesn't necessarily have any sex in it although this particular show is about societal cruelty to women. Torture porn. I googled it. No actual porno sites came up when I googled it. No actual porno sites came up when I subsequently googled food porn, beauty porn, fashion porn and hygge porn but it did when I googled porno porn, hardcore porn, product porn, alien porn, cocktail porn, love porn, soft porn, free porn, war porn, video porn, internet porn, ad porn, consumer porn and interestingly Quorn porn. As in the meat substitute Quorn. By this point I had completely forgotten what started this all and ended up buying a powder called mucuna pruriens on a sort of health guru former movie star website for £35 that's supposed to help me focus more and also release some dopamine in my brain so that I won't need to do scrolling quite so much.

This is when I decided it might be wise to spend the rest of my work day at the library.

I like the library. I sit there and mostly do what I would do at home except I don't have all the home distractions. It's very quiet. You're not allowed to talk – no one speaks. At all. Everyone there is there to do work. Reading and writing work. That's all people do at this library, and they mostly do it Very Seriously, as if people's lives depend on it. And maybe they do.

On this particular day, I was at a desk next to a woman who had taken lots of books out. She was writing, probably about the books she had taken out. This woman next to me, she was so focused. And her face was so relaxed. She seemed so happy working, doing her work.

I wasn't working. I was being nosy.

I looked at what books she had, the lady next to me, and read their spines. She had:
Women in Ancient Greece

The Greek Myths
Heretical Hellenism
The Cult of Divine Birth in Ancient Greece
Sexualities in Anthropology: A Reader
Why Men Love Bitches: From Doormat to Dream Girl

I didn't have any books at my little section of the long desk, not even a notebook. I thought about taking out a book, but the one I wanted wasn't available and anyway, this library doesn't let you take books home and I was only going to be there for the afternoon. All I had were some tabs open on my internet browser which included:
Google Search for 'silk or wool duvet allergies better'
10 best anti-allergy pillows
Easy Fish Stock Recipe
Google Search 'what to make with fish stock'
Google Search 'does pain in my right armpit mean I have cancer'
Google Search 'early warning signs for Alzheimer's mid thirties'
The Reformation clothing shop homepage
Wikipedia entry 'The reformation'
Google Search 'How to be more productive'

Okay. Here's a story.

I read the news before I go to sleep because at least then I can justify the nightmares and insomnia

Here is another story.

I would consider getting plastic surgery if it meant I could be on a TV show. I would consider plastic surgery without the being on TV part.

Here is another story.
I have had Botox in my jaw to help with my temporomandibular disorder – TMJ – which is just a fancy way of saying teeth grinding and jaw clenching and also between my eyebrows to help with my wrinkles and it cost £885

Here is another story.
I spent 6% of my total earnings from last year on this Botox. The effects of Botox last for four months, which is 33.33% of the year.

Here is another story.
Totally worth it.

Because if you start to think about life in percentages, it can be hard to feel like anything is worth it all. Like is there any real purpose to what I'm doing or saying in this very moment … and from there it's just really easy to get into one of those crises of what exactly is the point of anything, we're all just going to die anyway and let's be honest, there probably isn't an afterlife so this is all there is right? And who has time for that.

By the time I was born my Zayde, which is what I called my Grandfather, had lived most of his life. He had lived 88% of his life to be exact.

That meant that there was only 12% of his life left for us to get to know each other. Which was almost exactly ten years. I spent ten months of those ten years being a blob, then I spent the next two months being a blob with a personality. I don't really remember much of him during the next three years but when I was four and he was seventy-seven he used to play a game with me that I do remember. He would ask me "who are you" and I'd reply, in a sort of half giggle half delighted scream "I'm Jessica your granddaughter, who are you?" and he'd reply "I'm Mayer, your Zayde". And then he'd call me a sheyneh maidel and give me a dollar or a small piece of chocolate, or something.

After Zayde died, he'd come to me in my dreams and I'd say "Who are you?" and he'd say "I'm Mayer". And then he'd tell me not to worry. It was the same every time. Don't worry. There's nothing to worry about.

He turned up in all sorts of places, after he died. Once I had a dream about boarding school and there was Mayer, telling me not to worry.

And I had a dream where I was being chased by a serial killer through a field of orange flowers and Mayer was standing in the field telling me not to worry as I ran past.

There was the dream where I was being crushed by a subway train, but I was also kissing Jared Leto from *My So-Called Life*, Mayer poked his head out of the window of the subway carriage and yelled "Don't worry!"

I went to visit him after he died. I whispered into his stone that I wasn't worried.

But I lied.

I've not been dreaming much recently. Or at least I can't remember them if I am. I'd say, on the days when I can sleep at all, that I usually sleep between six and eight and a half hours, which is between 25-33.33% of the day. That leaves between 66.66 and 75% of the day awake. Which by all intents and purposes is most of the day.

During that time awake, I often feel I accomplish very little. My boyfriend, he's always working. I feel like he works all the time. He works more than he hangs out with me. He even works on vacations. He just always seems to have something to work on. And when he's not working, he's always got something else he's filling his time with. Never idle. He gets annoyed that I don't seem to have a good work ethic. He never says it in so many words, but that's what he implies. That it's my own fault that I can't seem to get anything done and that reflects badly on me as a person. Not working makes me a bad person. But when he implies things like that, it usually has the opposite effect of motivating me to be better at working … what's the opposite of motivate? Debilitate? Demoralize? Detonate?

A friend of mine bought me a timer that looked like a peach. It's supposed to be a tomato I think but she thought the peach one was cuter. She bought it for me because she's encouraging and kind and we had basically downed tools one Thursday afternoon and gone for a beer to talk about productivity and how hard it is to be productive, and she was telling me all about this magical timer. And then the next time we hung out, she gave me the peach. She was so excited, her eyes were actually twinkling, she said it really helps her and that it would definitely help me work, but it didn't. It just sat on my desk taunting my lack of productivity until I had to throw it away.

But I don't like throwing things away because what if it turns out in the future I will want it. And it was a gift. So, I didn't actually throw it away, I put it under the bed with my exercise stuff and shoes. And the journal I bought that was supposed to help me schedule my time better. And a photo of my Zayde's daughter. His first child, who I guess is technically my aunt.

But my grandmother isn't her mother.

So maybe she's my half aunt? She's 50% my aunt.

But also, she is forever five years old, because that's when she died.

Five years is 14% of my life. She was 7x younger than me when she died.

I don't remember the name of this girl in the photo, my long-lost half aunt, but I call her Esther.

When I was quite little, I thought Esther was just literally lost. I used to dream up stories about how Esther got lost. Like the time she and Zayde went horseback riding and Esther's horse ran off with her on it and no one could find her. Or the time she was exploring a mountain on skis and a helicopter came and Esther just grabbed onto the little dangly ladder and got whisked away into the sky.

Right around the time Mayer died, I believed that one day when I was older, at least sixteen or so, I'd go off on an adventure and use this photo to find Esther.

Of course I knew that there was no Esther. Because that's not her name. My long-dead baby half aunt.

I don't really look at the photo much.

I do look at it more than I use the peach timer though. Even though recently I feel like I have become increasingly unproductive. I feel like I'm just waiting for things to happen. I feel like a sitting stone. Or a standing stone. More like a standing stone. No one really knows why standing stones are there, do they. They just stand. In a field. Sometimes in a circle but not always. That's what I feel like.

Heavy.

Unchanging.

Gray.

Even when I do things that are supposed to be light, I feel heavy. Like even when I'm jumping. And I do a lot of jumping.

I found a person this one time while I was scrolling a couple of years ago who recommends jumping. For health. Before I found her, I didn't know that there could

be so many different types of jumping. There are so many types of jumps.
There are squat jumps and lunge jumps and jumping rope and high knee jumps and box jumps and boxing jumps and ski jumps and skier jumps and tuck jumps and split squat jumps and pulse jumps and car jumps and flying jumps and that's to name just a few.
I do so much jumping because I feel like jumping helps me to be better. In the day. In my life. It's like being early, it's like the buffer window. It … I don't know … mitigates.

But also, I do the jumping because I sort of hate myself.

I mean, everyone sort of hates themselves a little bit, right? But I am particularly good at finding new and creative ways to hate myself. So I jump because I hate myself but it also sort of helps me not hate myself so much and that's okay right, that's my privilege to do that and I do mean privilege, I am aware it's a result of that but allowing for that, I think it's okay.

I think that we can do things for more than one reason and I think those reasons can actually be fundamentally opposed to each other sometimes.

Like, I didn't really want to meet Harriet that day but also, I did.
I wanted to meet her because I knew that I wouldn't get what I wanted if I didn't meet her.
But of course, I couldn't really say what I wanted in the meeting with her because if I said what I actually wanted

in the meeting then I definitely wouldn't have gotten what I wanted because what I really wanted was for her to want me to make the work I wanted to make and for her venue to want to give me the resources to make it and then to make sure that the patrons of the building wanted to see this work I was working on.

But.
That isn't how this works.

In this place we live, and maybe also in places other than this place we live, we can't often say the things we really mean. Or ask for the things we really want. People don't respond well to it. People don't like needy people. People like busy confident people. But not too confident. People don't like people who Come On Too Strong.

And as a result, in this place we live and almost certainly in other places, I think people who make things often end up on the back foot and the people who sell things have the upper hand. Which means that in my meeting with Harriet, I was on the back foot. I didn't understand that phrase, back foot. Until I did a couple months of boxing. I was actually okay at it, so I kept it up, but eventually you have to fight someone in a ring and I got punched in the face when I was literally on my back foot. So I stopped. Because I don't want a broken nose. With Harriet, I was on the back foot because I didn't know what she was looking for, what she wanted and there was at least an 89.4% chance she wasn't going to tell me, whereas she knew exactly what I wanted even though I couldn't really actually say it too directly because I have a hard-enough time not coming on too strong as it is.

I still had five minutes left before Harriet was going to turn up. For our meeting that she was already technically thirteen minutes late for but only eight minutes past the buffer zone. That she had rescheduled three times before and that was going to be an initially pleasant but ultimately unsatisfying experience that would leave me with something literally unforgettable. In a bad way, the worst kind of way, in a way, because when you hear it, you're probably going to be like, that's not even that bad.

I googled anxiety TMJ teeth clenching best pillow
I googled mouth pain cheeks not TMJ tongue sore cancer
I googled braces to help TMJ and overbite more defined jaw
I googled reset diet lose weight fast
I googled what jobs can artists do career change
I googled what did Penelope really do while she was waiting Odysseus.
I googled can you have an acting agent and a writing agent who are the same person
I googled the names of six more successful artists than me with the phrase bad reviews

I went back to the crossword, didn't know the answer and put my phone down and closed my eyes for two seconds. I open them and I scroll some more and people people people people just keep talking talking talking talking and Shut up.

Just shut. The Fuck Up.

Stop talking. No one gave you the right to talk. It's not your right to say whatever the fuck you want whenever you want to.

WE ALL HAVE FUCKING OPINIONS.

Tell your mom. Or your friends.

Your opinion is not special.

I felt something in my chest. I feel something in my chest a lot. It feels like a bottle that is going to explode. It's probably a tumor.
I feel like I'm going to cry.

I always feel like I'm on the verge of crying.
It's really embarrassing. I'm a person in my thirties, pretty far into my thirties or at least half way through them, who cannot control my emotions.
Which isn't okay.
Especially in work contexts.
But also in social contexts. Life contexts.
It's hard to win an argument if you start to cry mid-way through it. For example.
It's all the time, not just sometimes.
I just … I cry.
I cry when I'm bad at things.
I cry when I don't get my own way.

I cry when I'm frustrated or angry or tired.
I cry when I'm nervous which is always.
I cry when mildly annoyed.
I cry when I read the news and listen to music and watch reality television.
I cry sometimes for no reason, like, I'll be fine and then I'll be crying and I won't really be able to put my finger on what it was that triggered it.
I cry when I think about my grandfather and my grandfather's daughter.
I cry when I think about my grandmother still in the apartment in the Bronx my father grew up in and my grandfather my Zayde died in and what her loneliness must feel like.
I cry when I think about loneliness in general.
I cry when I think about what Harriet said to me even though it's ultimately not a big deal even though it feels like it is.
I cried at Kate and Victor's wedding. More than once.
I cry when I laugh.
I cry on the tube. And the subway.
I cry in the motel.
I cry walking into the sea.
I cry and the music swells.
I cry and the camera slowly moves towards my face the light softening, my tears reflecting the exquisite pain of the world.

I cry and my suffering is rewarded with accolades and medals and statues and when I'm told what a good job I did, I cry again.

I sometimes wonder if I will stop crying if I have a baby. Because then the baby will cry instead. Maybe babies take all the sorrow from their mothers and that's why they cry all the time. Maybe parents in general transfer their sorrow to their children and that's why we are all born crying. Because we are passed the memories of our mothers and our fathers and our grandparents. Maybe that's why my Zayde forgot everything. Maybe he passed too much onto his children and his grandchildren. And when my sister, his fourth and last grandchild was born he gave her the final memories he had and then forgot. He forgot how to be an adult, he forgot how to eat, he forgot how to speak and he forgot his family. As far as we could tell.

I always imagine the child I have will be a girl. But of course, there is at least a 50% chance it will be something else entirely.
Perhaps I'll lay an egg and I will keep my egg in a special pouch around my neck – a pouch made of sheepskin, soft and warm and tenderly I will look after it while I prepare the tiny bed and room for whatever might hatch. And seven weeks and four days after the egg was lain, a crack appears and the soft scaly nose of my creature will smell the air for the first time and I will watch as it pushes its slippery body out of its former incubator and look at me with its huge yellow eyes and tiny green face and I will undoubtably feel a love I had not known I could feel.

And my little thing unencumbered by humanness will be scooped up into my cupped hands and brought up to my face and I will put them into my mouth where they will spend the night, a soft wet dark womb. And we will play a game where they will eat the plaque off my teeth and use my tongue as a surf board and I will rub their small purple belly as they sleep on a tiny satin pillow that doubles as a pin cushion.

And when we go out they will drape themselves over my ear like a brilliant cuff-ring, sticky hands suctioned on and ruby tongue reaching out to catch any wayward mosquitos in the warm night air.

My creature will have no gender, they will have no anxiety, they will not in their innocent perfection generate hang-ups that will lead to them dreaming up new and creative ways to hate themselves.

And they will not weep the tears of their ancestors, they will not cry all the time or even at all, they will not know crying. My creature, my child, will be free of that because my child will be a fucking lizard.

I didn't cry. Waiting for Harriet. Instead I continued to looked at my phone. I scrolled a bit, I looked in close up at the face of a beautiful reality TV star who scandalized the nation when it was revealed she had spent £25,000 earned from stripping on plastic surgery and then I googled 'movie stars plastic surgery' and scrolled through the before and after images. I would have her face, I thought when I looked at each photo. I would pay to have that face.

I was so engrossed in scrolling that when Harriet turned up I didn't even notice and it frightened me. Not frightened me like being basically certain I have Alzheimer's frightens me. Not like how climate change and the news in general frightens me. Definitely not as much as worrying that I won't really amount to anything, that I will die all alone with no teeth and no family frightens me. It didn't even frighten me as much as karaoke frightens me.

It more just caught me by surprise.

I was a little surprised, I jumped a very small bit when she said my name.

She said my name and apologized for being late. She said please call me Hen like the chicken, it's such a silly nickname isn't it but it's mine, thanks Mum and Dad. She said how great it was that we were finally able to meet up after all the cancellations how she's been so busy with everything and is still not very good at keeping up with schedules even though that's actually what most of her job is about. How one would think that doing her particular job and having two children and being in her mid no let's not kid ourselves her late forties that she should be an expert on this by now, she said, as she ushered me through the door into the hallway and then the elevator, down another hallway through another door down some stairs and into the public café where she said why don't you sit down tell me what you'd like to order, oh my god, you should have just waited in here it's so much nicer I'm such an idiot one day I'll be a real adult. At some point I must have said coffee with milk and I sat down in a booth at a table with some flowers on it near some big windows looking out into

the city and I looked at Harriet's outfit which was gray dark and light and expensive looking, her hair looked amazing and I took out my phone and I googled:
APC trousers resale wool dark gray
Celine jumper cashmere resale
Acne resale coat jacket
Isabel Marant resale leather trousers loose
Simone Rochas resale
Botox between eyes
What to do about jowls thirties no fillers
Why can't I sleep
Best way to get someone to give you what you want.

There is almost never an answer.
To the things I am looking for.
I mean there are too many, of course.

Harriet came back from ordering our coffees. And as this wasn't a meeting about anything in particular just working out whether my work would work in her place of work and if working together could work in the future, Harriet started talking again.

And I listened because I actually just want someone to tell me what I should be looking for or how to get to this place we are all meant to be going. I don't remember.

And nothing happens. Right? It's like I said

Nothing came of this conversation.

I continue to work. Harriet continues to work.

And this unremarkable thing she said to me, the thing I can't let go, it sort of felt like she thought she was doing me a favor. People have said things to me that have been much worse, like really mean.
I mean, people have always been mean. There must be 100,000 movies stories books articles historical documentations of cruelty. But this sort of I'm doing this in your best interest, this being cruel to be kind, this meanness in the guise of honesty – I feel like it's on the rise.
I've done it, I've been really fucking cruel under the guise of being honest. I have.

And I scroll I scroll I scroll and I see horrible things, sure, people saying flat out horrible things to each other. But also, there are things that look benign, these carefully edited insidious lovely pictures selling us a life we can't achieve.

My mind slips, it wanders off to a memory before this, years before, sitting in a motel or a hotel with an old style television with soft sounds radiating from the tinny speakers hidden in fake wood. I remember driving down big open roads across deserts rocky landscapes towards the credits.

But now it's Tuesday, it's Tuesday – which let's be honest is one of the worst days – but it's the day I went in for a meeting. I spoke to a woman who is slightly older than me. At the end of the meeting she said something that bothered me. It really bothered me. It attached itself to me like a weird little cartoon leech, that's sort of stuck on my heart, you know? It's so small and ridiculous you don't really think it's doing any harm but then occasionally, or like every time your heart beats, for example, you're like, ow!

So now I think of it whenever I do anything.

I'd be surprised if Harriet ever thought about it again.

I shift around in my seat, I move … I don't remember how to get to this place I'm meant to go so I'm just sort of moving. Moving just to move, just to do something.

Always jumping dancing packing unpacking travelling here there and somewhere else, not anywhere that glamourous, not like it looked when you just looked at someone else's photo of it.

I want to stay still for just a second. Stay here in this motel third floor walk-up in a city familiar but unplaceable I know I've been there before I just don't know when.

Kate and Victor weren't going to do a normal honeymoon. That's what they said in their speeches. They took six months off work. They were going to travel around. Just pack a small bag and go off to see the world. This was the start of their adventure. This is the start of the adventure of their lives. And of course by that they mean their trip but also their marriage.

They need to do this trip before the adventure of their marriage becomes the main adventure because once that adventure starts you can't take any other big trips. Ever. Again.

I am watching these two people speak in front of a crowd of two hundred and fifty of their closest friends and family. I watch people laugh and coo when man after man mentions how beautiful all of the prominent women at the wedding look and what a wonderful community of family and friends it is. But how well do we actually know each other, I think, trying to remember the name of the person across from me who I definitely met on the shared night out Kate and Victor had before their wedding.

They called it their Shen-dag. Like shin-dig, and like what you could sort of get if you crossed the words stag do and hen do …

I think they should have called it a Shag-do.

But the point is they wanted to break the rules, and do it together.
I mean, the sentiment was … it's actually a nice idea I think.

I wasn't sure where this was going. Not literally. Literally I knew we were going to do karaoke, on the Shen-dag. I hate karaoke.

It's more that I didn't know where this was all going to end up. I am singing. I am listening to someone tell the happy couple of all the things they had to look forward to. I am thinking about the fact that Kate and Victor would take photos of themselves in far-away places smiling on filthy trains and overcrowded buses as they um … they deliberately do things cheaply … What is that phrase. When you do that? It's not ghetto it's …

Slum.

They slum it, they will say they slummed it in order to have a real experience and then will look back at those times recount them in the pub and at barbeques at children's third birthday parties and think about how they experienced the real world, like the world they live in isn't real.

I am watching the screen with all my might, I look at the photo I sink into the story and I reach out over the balcony. The sea is shimmering, it's beckoning me and I think about how at the start of the story there's no wind, and all the men can't even get their boats out to sail to war and leave us behind until a young woman is murdered and we're left, picking up the pieces, waiting. And I can't imagine there ever not being wind here. The bright blue only broken by the reflecting sun. It's blinding, the sea. I swim out and panic I'm too far away. The sirens, they call to me and I can't ignore them. My feet are sunburned.

Harriet is telling me a story about a work on professional karaoke singers. The Birdcage I say. With what's his name? she says. Columbia Road I say, by the flower market. Right, the comedian, she says. Robin Williams I say. It's been taken over, she says, now it's just another anonymous pub. Also the other one I say. Nathan what's his name she says. They don't karaoke there anymore, I say. I love to sing. And I love Miami she says. I smile.

I'm tired of moving so I float. My goggles have water in them, I can't figure out how to make them seal properly. I put my head under to try to drown out the sirens, their cries. I have water in my ears and I worry about getting an ear infection. I get a lot of ear infections. A doctor once laughed and said he had never met someone older than eight who gets as many ear infections as I do. I thought that was a little mean.

Did you know that in Japan they have professional karaoke singers says Kate. The Birdcage says Victor. No, Japan says Kate. There are about thirty of us. My boyfriend also hates karaoke. He hates being the center of attention. It's another reason we will never have a wedding. It's another reason we never throw parties. He's there, but he's shrunk away. He is now a tiny ant or a little bee. A very small umbrella. A melting ice cube. He is anything but here anywhere but him.

Are you going to sing says Victor. Oh! You have to, you have to, you have to everyone has to. I look for my boyfriend but I can't find him. He's too tiny now and the light in the bar seems to be mostly UV. I don't really sing I say. I'm not good at it and doing things I'm not good at stresses me out.

I tried to learn French recently. It didn't go well. Learning is a lot harder when you aren't a child – my brain exercises are supposed to help with that but … It's not that I didn't try … I went to classes, I sat on my couch every day repeating French words back at the app in my phone. And I've watched a lot of French movies and I use mostly French skincare.

All the women in France have very nice skin according to my scrolling. Their skin is so nice they just don't really need to wear make-up. They're so low-maintenance! Like, the French woman in the 'Ithaca is Gorges' T-shirt, she actually says things like 'I just woke up like this'. Lots of these women apparently 'just wake up like this'. But behind every smiling face there's a strict regime and I get it, people don't like people who are high-maintenance, it's really cool and fun to be low-maintenance and make-up looks high-maintenance while skin care is basically invisible. And luckily there are lots of think pieces you can scroll through about how to be more low-maintenance-seeming and more French and it was from reading one of those think pieces that I arrived at my regime which is basically the exact same regime as the Ithaca is Gorges lady, so there's that.

*(Voiceover in French – not Jess's voice.)*

The first step in my regime is to clean my face.
I wash my face in a French way. I have watched a number of videos that a French woman put online about the correct way to wash your face, and I would now say that I might be an expert on French face washing.

To start, I spray special water from a bottle onto my face. For the PH balance. Then I apply my facewash to my face. I use a very gentle face wash that does not strip my skin of moisture. To have moisturized skin is to have beautiful skin. I want beautiful skin

I make little circles on my face and my neck spreading around the facewash. I am very fast and light with my fingers. I do this for a minute. Then, I take a damp muslin cloth and polish my skin with it and finally I wash my face with tepid water. I had to look up the definition of tepid. It means only slightly warm, or lukewarm and it is only used in relationship to liquids. Interestingly, in the definition on the internet, the sentence example they give is 'she soaked a flannel in the tepid water' which is what I was literally doing! Because muslin and flannel are interchangeable, at least when you are talking about a washcloth for your face. I found that amusing.

Once I have rinsed off my face wash, I dab my face dry with a towel. Just dab it though. We should treat our skin like silk. Like very delicate silk.

Once my face is dry, it's time to apply the product. I don't know why I say product as a singular because there are lots of products.

I use different product in the AM and the PM.

In the AM, I begin by using a toner. I apply toner by putting it onto pads and rubbing it onto my face gently. I'm not sure what toner actually does. But apparently it is to help my face receive the product. I found this confusing at first because technically toner is also a product. I then use a snail essence. It sounds gross, but it's not. Then I use two different serums – vitamin C for glow and hyaluronic acid for moisture. I rub it in my fingers and then I apply it in a similar way to the way I wash my face but with more vigor. I do the massage so my cheeks stay sculpted looking and I make sure to do my neck and jaw-line because apparently if you massage your jaw upwards you are 5% less likely to get jowls. And I really don't want to get jowls. I like my neck. It's not as long as the women who do the tutorials, and there isn't much I can do about that, but I still like it. The circular motion, where I massage round my eyes and forehead, is called swimming. I think that's funny because that's where my swimming goggles leave a mark. Incidentally, I have yet to find goggles that don't leave a mark and for a while I didn't go swimming because I was worried the goggles were making my eyes look old. But then I realized it was just aging.

Finally, once I have applied all the serum, I apply the moisturizer. I choose my moisturizer depending on what I am doing. If it is winter I use a heavy moisturizer, if it is summer I use a lighter one. If I am going out and going to wear make-up, I use a priming moisturizer. I warm the product in my hands, because cold moisturizer apparently DOESN'T WORK. I do the same face massage I already did, but even more vigorously. I make sure not to forget my neck.

I put on eye cream. Just dab dab dab dab dab dab dab dab dab dab dab. Dab dab dab dab dab dab dab dab dab dab dab dab dab. Until it is all absorbed.

Finally, if I am going out in the daytime, I apply 50spf UVA and UVB protected sunscreen. Not if I am just sitting at home. My moisturizer has sunscreen in it. But if you are at the computer you should use sunscreen apparently. I read that somewhere.

In the PM, my regime is slightly different. Three times per week I exfoliate with acid. I put the acid on my face and leave it there for ten minutes. The acid makes the top layer of my skin come off to reveal newer, younger, fresher, more beautiful skin underneath.

When I am done exfoliating, or if I haven't been exfoliating after I have washed my face, I put on some prescription Retin-A. I use the Retin-A so I don't get hormonal acne. Or that's what I tell the doctor. It's half true. I also use it because vitamin A stops your skin from aging.

After I apply the Retin-A, I use something called a dermaroller on my face. A dermaroller is a small roller that has 580 0.75mm needles on it. I roll it over my skin, up and down, side to side and on the two diagonals. The dermaroller makes little injuries on my skin. The injuries make my skin produce more collagen. Young skin has lots of collagen. Collagen is the opposite of gravity. And gravity is the enemy of our faces. ALSO! The dermaroller makes your skin 200% more likely to absorb the product.

When I finish dermarolling, I apply my serums. Sometimes I'll do a mask. I love masking. I love making the most out of all the steps. You just sit. With the mask on. For like forty minutes. It's so relaxing. But most of the time, I'll just put two different oils on and then go to sleep.

The whole process, all the steps in the regime … it really doesn't take that long. It takes much less time to do it than it does for me to tell you about doing it.

And my skin looks plump. That's a thing. Plump skin.

Beautiful skin is plump skin. It is important that if you want to appear very low-maintenance and not wear make-up but still look great in the photos you post for people to see when they are scrolling, having plump skin and visible necks is a must. No matter what your age.

*(End speaking in French.)*

I initially wanted to learn German. But French is more beautiful. And that's important.

But the reality is that I stopped going to the French classes and practicing because I was bad at it, even though I know that the way to get good at it is by going to the classes and practicing.
But I don't want to do things I'm bad at. I spend so much of my day hating myself already, you know?

I'm not really bad at anything except scheduling, Harriet says with a laugh. I'm trying to stay still but I can't stop moving, twitching. Harriet is still talking about something maybe her children? Or her haircut? I can't focus I want to take my phone out and just have a little look. A short go at my crossword or check the news or my emails anything so I don't have to listen just get out of this situation I really don't want to do the karaoke.

I have actual nightmares about karaoke, I'm at a bar and my name gets called and I stand up and I don't know the words or the tune to the song and everyone laughs, they're throwing tomatoes, they're throwing peanut butter sandwiches and fish soup at me. There is a piano player and music from a speaker and they are clashing and no sound comes out of my mouth and when it does it sounds like some … animal, dying … in a drain. And my Zayde sticks his head round the side of the piano and tells me I don't need to worry and I JUST DON'T BELIEVE HIM ANYMORE.

Why did you leave us? I yell to him. We needed you. Why did you forget us? Please come back. I'll be better, I'll be a better child I won't cry even I'll just listen and I'll let you give me all of your stories I'll take them from you if your promise to not forget me.

We can't undo this he cries, as begins to play the intro to Meatloaf's 'I Would Do Anything For Love'. I can't undo what happened. I can't undo what happened. I can't undo what happened.

I hear my name. Kate's calling it. My Zayde is calling it. Duncan slaps me too hard on the back and woofs and rubs the top of my chest like I'm a dog.

Sorry mouths Kate. She's smiling.

I hear my name again, the Karaoke MC is calling it.

Oh fuck.

I am alone.

I have no faith but long before that my God abandoned us. We are all alone. We were left on our own to survive with light shoved into glass jars and like ceramic pots to guide us. I learnt this. Didn't I learn this somewhere? The light it wasn't meant to be contained, we didn't know,
I didn't know how to hold it and it fractured, it died,

exploded, scattered into tiny shards, that's all that we have left so we spend our lives desperately trying to collect them, to grasp onto something meaningful in a world where there is sometimes only darkness shining through our screens.

The heroes of my childhood are liars. They are selfish, they are made in the image of a God who is vengeful and angry.

I am alone at the table, on the makeshift Karaoke stage in the crowded bar the wedding venue the motel room window the beach looking out at the endless sea.

I am looking out across the darkness the blue the crowd to find you but you don't exist.
Or you do, but only in my head.
The seams are splitting in my imagining of you and you are whoever I want you to be.
You are there behind the screen, you are there behind the lights. I don't have any photos of you but I will remember what you look like in my mind. Put your hand through the screen.
I want you to catch me if I fall.

I look out into the audience.
Harriet's mouth is moving but I hear no sound coming out.
My grandfather is making drinks at the bar and he yells to me that everything is going to be okay.
My lizard crawls from my ear into my hair because the lights are too bright the music too loud.

My boyfriend is gone, he evaporated, he turned into a fruit fly and was eaten by a spider and Victor's phone is up in the air documenting this moment live for everyone he doesn't know.

I was born with fear. I inherited it. I am scared of everything.

Harriet, Hen, Hennie like the chicken, laughs, She says I can't imagine you being scared of anything. Maybe that's your problem.
Some people just don't like women with no fear. Some people just don't like women who talk about themselves.
You're just … you a lot. You know. You're a whole lot of everything. I love it, but it can be unpalatable for some people.
I love your work, and I'd love to work with you to make that work work for here, I just don't think right now it would work with the kind of work our patrons, customers really, are into. One day I'm sure this will work, if you become someone – and your kind of work becomes something – that works for more people. You know?

I wish I had a real baby with me. My eyes are stinging and that familiar feeling of needing to explode is moving up inside me and I pretend to yawn so I can justify these tears here. These tears seem inappropriate. It is inappropriate for me to feel what I am feeling isn't it. I feel like someone is going to have to peel me off the floor.

Harriet keeps talking as Meyer delivers me my coffee and with a wink he hands me a mandel bread under the table and says es a bisel sheyneh maidel.

Harriet doesn't notice. She is still talking.

She talks about her husband.

She talks about her children.

She talks about her job, her colleagues and her projects.

She talks about her last project – the one I couldn't remember. The one I wouldn't look up as I waited for Harriet to arrive almost half an hour after we had arranged to meet just so she could tell me I was unpalatable … This work, it was by a man named PAUL.

PAUL! HIS NAME WAS PAUL. I feel relieved that she told me his name and I didn't have to look it up and now I will remember it forever PAULPAULPAULPAULPAUL is a middle aged man who makes work that sort of rips stuff off of more experimental workers and then claims he's made some sort of new discovery. He's a little bit like someone who wishes he had been in a punk band but was never actually brave enough charismatic enough to do it and even though now that he's older and does something else and never actually was part of this scene he's so obsessed with he likes to tell everyone he has kept his "punk fuck everything fuck everyone I can do whatever

the fuck I want spirit" even though I'm not 100% sure
that's really what punk was even about.
I don't think Paul is malicious. I think he's just…
I don't think Paul ever really thinks about it. You know?

Maybe that's the problem.
Maybe we don't think about it.
Or maybe we think about it too much but don't do
anything about it.
Or maybe we do things about it but we shouldn't. Maybe
we should let other people do things instead. Make some
room for other people.

I don't know what the right thing is. I don't know what
I'm allowed to do.
I can see where I need to get to but there isn't a clear path.
I'm not sure I have the right to feel how I feel and I keep
looking for things to distract me from feeling anything at all.
I think about shoes.
I read about Penelope.
I look at photos of Kate and Victor and the beautiful French
woman.
I watch Duncan lean in and put his hand really high up the
waitress' leg as she squats to take his order and I feel a little sick.

The title of my song comes on and the intro starts to play.
I am sweating.
I pray to the God of my childhood the God I don't believe
in I say please God let this be a dream let me wake up
from this I really don't know how I get myself into these

situations it's not even a big deal it's just a fucking meeting,
it's just karaoke I am holding the microphone at the wedding,
maybe I've had too much to drink to be doing this.
This isn't suffering … People really suffer all the time. This
is just … this is just … I can't find the word.

I'm probably dying. I can't remember words anymore
because I definitely have a brain tumor.
I am at my computer. I am at the library and the people
next to me are all wearing noise cancelling headphone so I
open my mouth and let out a squeak. Everyone is working
away around me and I'm squeaking and they don't notice
so I keep going til it becomes this low guttural cry. I am
definitely dying of a brain tumor or lung cancer or some
rare tropical disease that has made its way to the place
where I live. I am going to die and no one will even notice
because they are all wearing headphones. They won't even
hear when the bomb goes off.

I'm not going anywhere but I can't stop moving. It's a
loop. I can't finish the fucking crossword puzzle and I
don't want to search for the answer because I know the
god damn word it's in there somewhere. Harriet hasn't
arrived yet. That hasn't happened yet.
I don't know what she is going to say yet, but you do. And
it's not a big deal is it?

I google why can't I let things go
I google why do I only remember bad things
I google is generational trauma a real thing

I google best dress to wear to a stylish wedding as guest
I google flights to LA
I google am I having a nervous breakdown
I google Alfred Hitchock
Jean Luc Goddard
David Lynch
The Hours
The Odyssey. I google
Noah Baumbach
Neil La Bute
Nicole Kidman Crying
Meryl Streep Crying
Brigitte Bardot Crying
Beyonce Crying
Salma Hayek Crying
Grace Kelly Crying
Julianne Moore Crying
Jennifer Lawrence Crying
Halle Berry Crying
Gwenyth Paltrow Oscars Crying
Claire Danes Ugly Crying
Beautiful women ugly crying
Oscars for people who gained weight for role crying
Sharon Tate crying
I want to go swimming.

I start to cry a little bit. I can hear my lizard shifting its little suction feet around in my hair.

The intro is nearly finished, the first line of my song appears on the screen.

I pull out my phone and I buy a pair of jeans that I definitely can't afford.

I stare at my computer and wish I'd taken out a book.

I think about how I shouldn't have bought those jeans. I think about how I won't really be able to return them because they are coming from America and by the time they get here, the return period will be over. I hope they fit. I hope I didn't get that wrong.

Harriet. She gets things wrong too. That's what she says to me in the meeting. She has a lot going on, this lady. In her life. She has a lot to say, and I think am I really are we really here?

But this is where I am.

I'm at a motel. It's like I'm in a movie. I mean, the room looks like every motel room you've ever seen in every movie. If you were to close your eyes and imagine a motel room in LA or anywhere in America really, whatever you're imagining is what this room looks like. Wood paneling. Seventies wallpaper. Dim orange lights. Brown bedspread to cover the stains of the lives of whoever stayed here before. Throw in some worn out shag carpet for good measure.

The television hums and I sit on the side of the bed wearing a white tank top and underwear with lace detailing around the legs. Maybe the underwear has small flowers. Maybe it doesn't. My legs are slightly open, elbows resting on my knees, head in my hands. The neon glow from the motel sign blazes into the room through the thin gossamer curtains and we pan around me my arms my back the top of my head close up onto my dirty finger nails.

And we've seen this a million times, I've seen this a million times, and I always hoped my story would be somehow … I always thought …um …

I don't know. One with backing dancers … one with true glamour … one with drama.

I take out my phone and I want to search for an answer but I am having trouble remembering why this is where I am, what part of this journey I am on what scene I am in and I can't seem to remember how we got here. Am I waiting or am I travelling?

I look across the table at Harriet. She's still talking. I do that thing that I do where I smile and inhale at the same time in an effort to make myself seem more engaged than I actually am.

Although in reality it probably reads more like I'm not really paying attention. Which is true. I've never been a good liar.

What do you do? She says. Hen says.

Excuse me?

I meant what are you doing?

Here?

Now. She says now, here and now but I don't hear.

What are any of us doing here? There are a bunch of things that were out of our control like who our parents are, where we were born, our race, our sex, our class, our gender and whether we identified with it, our sexual orientation and what teachers we were assigned at school and how good our school was and what neighborhood it was in and how the world treats us because of those things. And then we just made some choices. And some of them are good. And some of them are bad and at the time we think we are making the right decisions but looking back we realize they were wrong but sometimes we're just too stubborn to admit that so we sort of carry on even though we feel like we could be doing something else or that we could be somewhere else or that we could be someone else.
I feel like I've lived a thousand lives. I don't know if I am the one on the journey or the one doing the waiting. Either way, for twenty years this hole has been growing inside me and it will keep growing and one day I'll die, but before that I'll forget all of this, my brain will give up, it will just stop wanting to remember. Nothing that bad has even happened

to me, my life is not the life of my Grandfather but it's like someone is sucking all the oxygen out of me with straws and to make it worse the straws are plastic and they keep throwing the straws away and they end up in the ocean and the beautiful seabirds eat them and die.

And it might be the fizzy wine going to my head but I think to myself, I should say this. I should say this now. I should say this out loud. Mayer is stretched out on the bar, he winks at me and takes a shot of whiskey, he smells some bread he rolls onto his back and closes his eyes and my lizard moves from my hair to my shoulder down my arm and into my handbag. It's too much for them now the raging storm shaking the frame of the building and lashing against the single paned motel window.

I stand up in the room and walk around the bed, the hum of this huge ugly city sounds like poisonous fumes and I think this isn't what I thought this would be like. Where's my pink house next to the Hollywood sign with its viewing window into my make-up getting ready room so my fans could adoringly watch me? Where's my champagne and my $5000 dress and my fucking Oscar?

I pull on some jeans, it's so hot that I struggle to get them on, the ceiling fan barely stirs the air … I walk out of the room on to the outdoor motel walkway and a kid in exactly the same outfit as me is doing a dance by themselves with headphones on and I think to myself I've been here before I've seen this all before.

And I walk.

I mean now, Harriet says.

I am just working I say … I've just. Gosh, I can't seem to think about the details of what I've been doing… that's so funny, it's like … it's just … I mean. I've just been working. All the work, all the working days have sort of … um … blurred.

We all raise our glasses at the end of Duncan's speech, we are on this journey with them we are all going to go on this journey with them. We are all going places! WHERE ARE WE GOING? I yell. WHERE IS THIS PLACE? WHY DON'T WE KNOW WHERE IT IS?

I've been lost. I've been lost at sea or I've been waiting for your return. I think to myself that everyone in this story will die.

I am standing next to the water. An ocean or a lake or a river or just a manmade Coy pond in the grounds of an overpriced wedding venue somewhere out there beyond the edge of the city.

The storm is coming. Or the storm is happening. Or has just happened. There is electricity rolling down through the trees from the sky and everything that was dry was wet and everything that was wet is flooded. I am standing facing waves and undercurrents facing into a history shining out of a light. A single ray cuts through this storm before we are pummeled by the wind, I stand my eyes open raindrops searing onto my irises and pupils and I begin to walk into the water, I allow the storm to build around me to sink into my body osmosis of liquid and solids and particles moving around and outside becoming inside and my eyes are wide open they are wide open and I pry my lips apart and cold salty wet rushes into my insides lunges and stomach cervix uterus I become the sea I become the storm I am standing on the beach I am standing on the banks I am standing in the ocean floating in the waves pounding down onto the surface of the earth and I lay down on the empty highway the desolate boulevards lined with disused cinemas and unpatroned bars and convenience stores that sell only cigarettes that no one even smokes anymore the road slick with gas or petrol mixed with misty humid air and reflecting bright red signs selling love and women and company and I sharply inhale the fumes the sea the algae on the surface of the lake.

I inhale. I raise my glass, everyone in the room is looking at me. I am the storm. I am the sea. I am the loving you are seeking in the dark theatres all alone. I am the road taking you out of this fucking city. All these drunk blurry faces, basically everyone is crying from the last speech, the words come onto the screen and the little bouncing karaoke dot starts moving. Everyone takes their phones out, mouths agape and I bring the microphone up to my mouth and I say:

Somewhere in the world a bomb goes off.

Somewhere right now a rape is happening.

Someone is getting married. Not you guys. Someone else.

A baby just died.

An old woman has drowned herself in the bath.

A first birthday party is ending with too much cake.

A boat has gone off course and it will take ten more years before its captain will return home.

An island is overrun by puppies.

I wish you the best of luck, I really do. I think you are good together.

But look, it's quite possible you won't go anywhere. It's quite possible you will stay here forever trapped in this moment. Just looping through it. Never being able to leave, never being able to live up to all this. Perhaps this is the final destination, perhaps there just isn't anywhere to go from here.

People travel all the time, people are going places right now.

Or wish they were. Or maybe wish they weren't.

People are forced to go on journeys for all sorts of reasons. Some people don't even know they are being forced, they think it's a choice to take these journeys.

Right now, someone is walking over sand towards a body of water and they are going to walk into the water and no one will ever see them again.

Right now, a memory is fading away into nothing and in a week someone will bring that memory up and you'll have to lie and pretend that you remember that it wasn't gone.

Right now a drone has killed someone. And now.

And now.

I stole that part from someone else. The part about the drone. I stole that from a writer I like.

Maybe this is as good as it's going to get for you. Maybe it's okay if you stay here forever, live in this moment and never go anywhere again.

Because … none of us really matter, ultimately, do we. More to the point, we're probably part of the problem. So maybe you should just stay here.

At this moment right now this moment right here this is when I remove my mouth.

I remove my mouth I simply detach myself, disown it. I press the rest of my face into the pillow knuckles gripping hard on the microphone as my mouth wanders off into the crowd.

I press so far down that I lose track of what my mouth is doing entirely. It could be doing anything it's lusty hot breathed mind of its own licking and sucking chewing and running off anything it can think to say.

It probably insulted someone. Maybe charmed someone else. I don't know. I missed that whole bit.

My eyes are shut tight I don't dare open them, and the tears are starting to drown my head, water is spilling out of my nose and ears down my chin and neck and breast bone, staining my dress. My mouth is sitting at a table laughing maniacally and with my eyes closed I reach through the darkness to find it to take it with me away from this place.

I can see without eyes. I can see everyone looking at me.

I can see you through all this darkness.

I don't need to open my eyes, I can see you even from here.

We walk hand in hand through this empty city, this city with what thousands with millions and millions of people in it, but for now it seems like there is no one.

Impossible that there is no one here but us, I think.

It's been a long time I say. But of course I am speaking to you through my mind because I have no mouth, it stayed behind at the bar at the banquet hall at the point the many points where it betrayed me.

Don't worry, you say. You don't have to be scared.

I'm worried I am going to forget all the good things and be stuck forever constantly searching I say.

You might, you say. You might.

And you let go of my hand and start to float first opaque then translucent just an outline, the edges dissolving, until there is nothing but the whisper of your voice on my cheek.

I open my eyes and stare out. My mouth is on my face I hold it tightly shut I can't trust it. My lizard climbs out of my bag onto my shoulder. I look out. I stare.

Don't worry you say.

Maybe I smile.